Jesus and Your Nice Church

Jesus and Your Nice Church

ED RICHTER

WILLIAM B. EERDMANS PUBLISHING COMPANY
GRAND RAPIDS, MICHIGAN

Library of Congress Catalog Card Number, 77-88077

Printed in the United States of America

Contents

A man should never be ashamed to own he has been in the wrong, which is but saying, in other words, that he is wiser today than he was yesterday.

— ALEXANDER POPE

Introduction

The pages that follow are crammed with complaints. Everyone likes to complain, of course. And in a sense I'm a complainer by nature — a rather finicky person who'd like to be able to demand perfection in others.

But if you'll forgive me my affinity for griping, and allow me a couple of hopefully valid points, I'd like to suggest that there just might be some value in this approach. The points are these:

1. The complaints are based on fact.
2. If you hold out long enough, they're followed by some concrete suggestions.

In other words, it's not all just nasty-nasty, negative, and non-productive. I spent more time trying to put together some possible solutions than I did chronicling the ills.

Still, the disease of an institutional church is portrayed rather thoroughly on these pages. (I refuse to be trapped into that *a priori* question, "What is the Church?" As it's used in this little book, the term means the institutional form. As long as it's there, claiming to house the "true believing church," it has to stand and take its lumps.) I'm speaking out mostly because I don't think you can attract sound practitioners of healing unless you convince them that something's wrong. And despite the fact that we've had many books that have concentrated on the wrongs, some of the most flagrant ills seem to have gone unnoticed. At least, they are still very much with us.

Because I talked this book out with colleagues, friends and enemies before I sat down to write it, I think I've already heard most of the objections to it. I know, for example, that I'd be much "more responsible" if I just forgot the complaints ("We all know they're there") and concentrated on some sound theologically oriented solutions.

I guess I would be more responsible that way. I know that's how many others do it, and they're responsible, aren't they? But are they effective?

And I think I know by now that the church has always had its problems, and always will — the implication being that we shouldn't waste our time on these. But this is my time on earth, and these problems are mine. And I have to deal with them.

I want to raise one fundamental issue in this book: Is the institution worth reforming? And assuming it is, shouldn't we be doing just that? I may be presumptuous to think that you've just given me two yes answers. But if you have, I'd like to toss in a few simple ideas in the interest of that reform.

I don't have all the answers, probably not even most of them. I haven't, for example, dealt with poor seminary training, although I've alluded to it. And I haven't even begun to sort out a meaningful theological debate (simply because I'm not a theologian or even a very good scholar).

But I have laid bare a few of the symptoms of trouble, and I've attacked them — even the unmentionable ones. And then I've tried to suggest ways in which the church could rid itself of those symptoms, at least.

The foundation for the book came from my employment by a national church body. Much of the material, therefore, is firsthand stuff. A lot of potential material was excluded, simply because I thought the writing would get redundant. And some complaints were left out in the interest of humanity: I just didn't see any point in raking a guy because he was sick, or because he made a single error of judgment. And I can't see the percentages in personal attacks, so I ignored that kind of thing, too.

I wish a few things more could have been included. My friend Jack M. MacLeod, for example, has written a brilliant satire on jargon, entitled "Sportsthought," in which he points out that the key to being bureaucratic in your language is to use the passive, and to avoid putting people into your writing ("It was felt . . . "). But the piece belongs to Jack.

I also wanted to include a tape-recorded transcript of a typical meeting, seminar or consultation. I could have, but I thought that was too much verbiage for the task at hand.

I owe some thanks here to MacLeod, to Bill Mooney and Stan Schmidt and others, who patiently read the manuscript. But my biggest thanks should go to a fellow I'll call the Rev. Mr. Sam. He's a church bureaucrat (in a different denomination), and he lives in a dream world in which a faithful church has great political power, and he's a part of it.

I didn't have the courage to disillusion him in person. So I wrote a book instead.

Jesus and Your Nice Church

Chapter One

It's a Different World, Jesus

NOW YOU SEE, JESUS, THERE ARE A FEW THINGS YOU don't seem to understand about today's world. In your day, you could gather a crowd and give a speech and turn people on with relative ease. But today you've got to take into consideration people's feelings, for one thing. And their busy schedules.

I guess people were a lot more willing to be confronted in your day, but it's all changed since then. They're sensitive now, Lord. Blame it on Western culture, or TV, or whatever, but the fact remains that they've become touchy about some things, and so you just can't go spouting off at the mouth.

We had this church-school teacher, for instance. She was a little inadequate to her task. Well, to be honest, she was awful. She didn't seem to be able to get the point of original sin, for one thing. She kept telling the kids that man was basically good, and not evil. The pastor knew all about it, and so did the superintendent and the committee. But they had to consider her *feelings*, Lord. I mean, after all, you wouldn't want us to go around *hurting* people, would you?

So we've had to let her teach for a while longer. But I wouldn't worry about her, because she's only ten or fifteen years away from retirement anyway, and we have a policy in that congregation. Besides, there's always the chance that her husband may change jobs in the meantime, and then she'd move on to another congregation.

It's that sort of thing I'm talking about, Jesus. And it isn't just laymen, either. Pastors have grown sensitive too. So you have to watch what you say around them also.

We've got a little scheme worked out to handle their feelings, though. You may recall the phrase "damning with faint praise"? Well that's the deal. You see, when you get a guy who's a lousy preacher, you can't just come out and say it.

But we've learned how to get the point across very well, I think. In fact, I'm rather proud of our little gimmick. It works like this:

Pastor Tom: "We're thinking of Joe T. over there for that new mission-pulpit spot. What do you think?"

Pastor Mike: "Well, he works *great* with young people, and I hear he's a tremendous administrator . . . . "

Pastor Tom (to himself): "Oh, he can't preach? Well, I know another candidate."

See what I mean? Without ever uttering one single syllable of condemnation, we've managed quite well to convey the thought. It's really quite Christian. I mean, you never hurt anybody like that.

We had another little case along those lines some months ago. It was a weekend seminar for church people, and they brought their kids along. Seems the local pastor we recruited to work with the senior highs wasn't doing very well. The kids were complaining that they weren't learning anything, and the parents were griping too. But we had this guy's feelings to consider, Lord.

I'm afraid we may have flubbed a little on that one. Not too badly, though. The kids may have suffered — there were forty of them — but we got through the whole weekend without ever annoying the culprit. What we finally decided to do was to let the situation ride. We figured that the kids would be going off to college pretty soon anyhow, and the chances were that they'd be moving on to other places. But we had to face the pastor later, and so we let him continue.

Prayer? Oh yes, you bet! We had prayers on the lawn during that whole seminar. A beautiful sight. You would have been proud of it. We had a big wooden cross erected out there, and the mountains in the background, and a lovely sunset. It was a real moving experience. Not as effective, I guess, as the pastoral prayer back home, when we dim the lights in the sanctuary, but we didn't have a P. A. system out there, and the clergymen couldn't get down into those lower stentorian registers. But we did have the mountains, and they added something. In fact, one guy even suggested that we get a mountainesque mural to hang up in the sanctuary back home — said it really gave it that nature taste. We're going to name a committee to study that one. I don't think it's such a hot idea, because some people like the seaside better than mountains, but we're going to give it to the committee anyhow, because this guy's a real hard worker in the church, and we don't want him to feel that we're ignoring his ideas.

You see, Lord, those Samaritans or whoever they were back in your day, well they were sort of hard-skinned. I mean they lived out there in the wilderness, without indoor plumbing, and I guess they got used to being treated roughly. But we've got bathrooms *and* powder rooms today, and you've just got to take it a little easier on people.

We are trying awfully hard to follow your example in other ways, though. Neatness, for one thing. We can tell by the pictures that you always kept your flowing hair well combed, and that you must have rinsed out that white robe every night, because it really shone. Well, we feel that way, too.

We had this kooky character who came into church one Sunday morning, right in the middle of the hymn of faith, and he was wearing a sport shirt.

He had a jacket on over it, and it was buttoned up at the neck, which I guess was okay, but he didn't have a tie on. Well, we've got a rather outspoken usher who was on duty that day, and he said later his first impulse was to refuse to let him in. He thought better of it, though, because it might have disturbed the congregation. Besides, I think the way we handled it was much more tasteful. We let him in (fortunately he slid into a back pew), and we all shook hands with him afterwards. Then we had the chief usher just whisper a hint to him.

He got the point, too, because the next Sunday he came back with a tie on. And he obviously hadn't been insulted. I mean we really made him feel right at home, letting him help serve the coffee that next week.

I'm not sure what has happened to him lately. He seems to have disappeared. Somebody said they thought he was going over to the Lutherans. (Frankly, I'm glad if he did, because the thing that annoyed me was that he was the only man in the whole congregation who had a mustache. Not the neat waxed kind, but a bushy thing. I think the guy had hippie tendencies or something. If he did, he'll feel much more at home with the Lutherans over there, because their pastor drives a sports car.)

Now I don't want you to get the impression that we don't confront people, Lord, because we do indeed. We can be pretty tough about it when the circumstances demand it.

We had this young girl who lived over there across the other side of town, and who came to church once in a while, and she seemed like a real nice kid. (To tell the truth, she was a real doll, with swinging hips, and several of the guys used to kid about it after church.)

Well, anyway, she got herself into trouble. You know, in a family way.

I guess she felt pretty guilty about it, because she went to see our minister. And he doesn't fool around! I mean when he's got a mind to say something, he just comes right out and says it!

He told her point-blank that she should make a public

confession of her sin before the church officers, and then we'd do everything in our power to help her.

Well, that's not pussyfooting around, is it?

Now this kid couldn't face you, Lord, and so she took off. Which was okay with us, because if she wanted to abandon her faith at a time like that, she deserved getting ostracized. The part that gets me, though, is that she or some of her friends started a rumor. A real nasty rumor, involving our choir director, who's a really stable family guy, with three kids and a wife who's been one of our real assets.

Well, the minister put his foot down. He said he would hear none of it, and that sort of squelched the rumor right there. The only thing is, the choir director's marriage broke up later that year. See how ugly talk can shatter the peace and unity of the church? The point is, though, that when it comes to real crisis, our pastor is a jewel. He kept that congregation humming just as smoothly as anything during that whole mess.

When you get right down to it, though, I guess the sort of crisis we face is nothing compared to what those pastors in the South must have had to deal with. I met one of them one day, while he was on a vacation up here, and he was telling me all about the race situation down there.

Lord, this guy really had his hands full! I mean down there, you see, those Coloreds were really trampled and all, and they had really big ideas about how to desegregate. Their motives couldn't have been all that pure, though, because he was telling me how they showed up one day, six of 'em, and what happened afterwards.

He was ready for them. The church officers had

called a meeting about it some weeks back, and they knew it was coming. So they roped off a pew near the back of the church, and just waited.

Well, the day they came the ushers politely handed them bulletins and pointed to the pew, and they all sat down. Now get this next point carefully, Lord, because it's important.

Not one person in that congregation said one nasty thing to those six Coloreds after that service! Not one! And those were people, don't forget, who'd been born and bred on that Deep South Tradition stuff. Now they didn't exactly embrace them, or anything. I mean, that would have been going pretty far, considering it was the South. But they talked, and some of them even shook hands, and one of the ushers even explained the service to them.

What I meant about their motives, though, was that they didn't settle for that. They didn't want to sit there and prove their point at all. They came right back the next Sunday! Not only that, but for four more Sundays in a row. The same six.

Well, what did they want? They had made their point and everything.

I tell you, I had a lot of sympathy for that pastor. He said he had all he could do for the next month or so, keeping his officers from really touching off a full-scale controversy in that church. Finally he had to agree with them, and they closed down the church to Negroes.

So I guess when you come right down to it, our troubles aren't really that serious.

Of course, we've been kind of lucky around here, because all the Coloreds in our area live over in what we call Darkietown, and they've got their own churches. Not that we wouldn't let them in here, of course. We would. But we're certainly not going to start raiding other congregations for membership, are we? I mean we're not exactly perfect Christians, but we know *something* about the faith.

You see, Jesus, this whole business of race and poverty and stuff is a lot more complex than it was in your day. Nowadays you've got ghetto riots and all sorts of anarchy. And crime in the streets! Those people just don't know the first thing about law and order.

Everybody knows they've got troubles, Lord. That's plain enough to see. But the way they're going about dealing with them is a travesty. They'll never make any progress at this rate. First of all, just when we get them started toward a good clean life they start looting and burning. I don't know *what* they want. And some of our politicians aren't being very helpful, either. They want to do something about their poor conditions, but the cost is just astronomical. Take rats, for example.

I heard of one rat-control problem that would cost something like seven dollars a rat to complete. Now that's a pretty expensive way of eliminating rats, isn't it? And welfare programs don't seem to help either, because those people will do anything to get free money — especially have babies.

Now we know enough about the Bible to realize a couple of important things about poverty, Lord. Like: God helps those who help themselves, and the poor we'll always have with us. So we're not panicky about all of this. What I think they really need, though, is faith. If they had some belief to fall back on, they'd be a lot better off.

You can tell that's a key item just by looking at them. I mean if you compare them with the people around here, you'll see the difference right away. All the people who come to our church are clean and well-dressed. Those other people don't even seem to care about cleanliness. And personally, I think that if you want God to help, you'd better start by washing your face once in a while.

We've got our international problems too. We know a lot of people are starving, but it's not as simple as it was when you just multiplied loaves and fishes. Those people in India, for example, will starve while they let those big fat cows trample all over the place. Now I think it's a real waste of money, Lord, to try to help those people unless they start helping themselves. They could start by eating those cows.

And this whole question of Americans feeding the world sometimes makes me wonder. There are other things involved, as you should well know. There's a limit to our resources, for one thing. If we just put all our farms into full-scale operation and started shipping food all over the place, we'd be broke in a year. And then who'd feed those people? So we've got to protect our economy, for their sake.

You see, Lord, it's just that things are an awful lot more complicated now. And even something as simple as "feed the hungry" has got to be studied in context.

But I don't want you to give up on us, because we are beginning to make some real progress. We're stopping Communism, we're fighting poverty, and we're passing new bills to give the Colored more privileges every year.

In our own church, we've had a Sunday morning study group going for nearly two years now. We started right at the beginning, with Genesis, and we're working our way right through your Holy Word, hoping to get some new insights for our day. We're into some of the prophets right now, and to tell the truth that gets kind of boring, but we have a pretty good teacher, and he's doing a good job of explaining it all to us, and I'll bet some of the guys will really benefit from this course.

So when you're tempted to start pressing us, Jesus, try to remember that we're really not standing still in all of this mess. It's just that these things take time, that's all.

Chapter Two But We Love Them, Lord

NOW YOU SEE, READER, I PULLED A NASTY TRICK with all that Jesus-and-me dialogue stuff, and I know you're chomping at the bit a little, because I exaggerated, and I oversimplified, and I caricatured the church and stereotyped all the Christians.

But before *you* start pressing, I'd like to say one thing in self-defense: those are the things that are happening. Those and a lot more. There *was* a suffering little girl who *was* great with child, and she *was* told to confess her sins publicly. And that Deep South pastor really exists, word for word.* His name—and all those names — are legion in our church.

And while the world erupts around us, that great institution we call the church seems to get more ingrown. The more it pronounces, the more it seems to lose its influence on society. The more it studies, the less it seems to care for action. The more it worships, the less it appears to listen to its God.

In truth, it is a mighty complicated world. But then again, it's a mighty complicated church structure, too. And a sick one. Nobody's got it diagnosed as yet, but the symptoms are all over the place: administrivia, church busywork, haughtily proud congregations, a God who's either dead or is Speaking To Us Through the Hippies, an old and creaky institution that pleads for reform but cites its would-be reformers as heretics, and a style of theological jargon that defies comprehension.

One of its most obvious symptoms, though, jumps right out at you from the printed page. It's the church's preoccupation with self-flagellation.

There's something mighty sick about a patient who keeps pleading with his physician to tell him how sick he is. "Just once more, doctor, please; tell me again how I'm dying."

And the church's appetite for hearing its own death knell is apparently insatiable. The books alone would top almost any snowy white spire: *Games Chris-*

*Yes, I cheated a little by fictionalizing some incidents and disguising them, but my purpose isn't to malign individuals. So if you think you recognize your congregation somewhere in these pages, remember that it isn't. The one I'm talking about is at the other end of the country.

tians Play, God's Frozen People, The Comfortable Pew, and so on. Christians — sophisticated ones, of course — sport them at all kinds of church-connected events. You'll find them upon the shelves in pastors' studys, in church libraries, in bookstores. You'll find them upon lips Presbyterian and Episcopalian and Pentecostal. The only thing you won't find them upon is acted.

But they're discussed, studied, pondered, worried over, read and re-read, and even occasionally condemned. The point is that they're there, and that's where it's happening, friend, right there on those sophisticated pages where it tells us again how an unfaithful church is a dying one, again, and again, and again . . . .

Of course, there are some critics who can't write very well, so they take to the lecterns. And they speechify grandly on the same theme, and the church asks for more.

I attended a meeting at which speaker after speaker played the same tune. Applause followed applause, knowing glance followed knowing glance, and those who hit the hardest got the standing ovations. One woman finally got it all figured out. "I guess," she said, "it's better than having to *do* something."

Her point was solidified an hour or so afterward, when one speaker dwelt on the inevitable meeting-ending theme, "Where Do We Go From Here?" Her mistake was that she offered concrete proposals for action. Several of them. She got polite applause.

What makes a church seek out its critics and laud them? Is it a need for reformation, deeply felt? Or is it an incurable disease, deeply penetrating? Is it guilt feelings or masochism?

At the other end of the spectrum is the churchman who sees Glimmers of Hope Shining Through a Very Confused Situation. "You know," he says knowingly, "the church has always had its difficulties. It's always been in trouble. It's always been guilty of being unfaithful."

Then the patient, prophetic smile crosses his lips. "And I suppose we'll always have our problems. After all, man is man." *His* answer is Faith, spelled, "I Am Too Old and Tired To Fight."

He'll also tell you with another smile — this one touched with pride — how the church is Serving People through all of this. "Still," he says, "I see people being ministered to by the church. I see the church doing things." At least one inference is plain: the patient may be stricken, but he's still twitching a toe or two.

And then his clinching argument: "Some really great things are happening in the church. We're really facing challenge." This one translates out to a new consultation planned for early next spring, or a reorganized committee and a new chairman.

What's missing here is the one ingredient that Jesus and the early church had going for them and the one tactic that Christians have used successfully for centuries. It's called confrontation.

Now as a theologian, I'd make a pretty poor shortstop. But I do know that Jesus calls Christians to act, to do things, and not just to ponder them. And it's personal responsibility that's at stake. But we've lost that angle somewhere.

Along the path from persecution to affluence we stumbled over a shrub called good-feelings, and we stopped to partake of its fruit, and we have become tainted by it.

Down the road from movement to institution, we have hitched a ride on a streetcar named Comfort, and it has taken us past the reality of the slum and into the beauty of the suburb, and we can't find our way back.

Somewhere along the line, the God-becomes-man realism has become the God-is-our-type-of-man myth, and myths aren't to be tampered with.

A good church school teacher in New England demonstrated it well. She was telling about the Christmas story, and she had her little toddlers come up to the crib, and "wrap the baby Jesus in beautiful clothes, and put him in the sweet-smelling hay."

The beauty of the Christmas story, it would seem, is that Jesus was born in pretty cruddy surroundings, and the hay probably smelled of manure. After all, it was to common men that He was born, wasn't it? But this woman had de-manured the hay, and the common dress of the common child became "beautiful clothes," and the story took on a new meaning.

"But didn't you make the point that this was the disenfranchised family?" I asked.

"Oh, heavens no," she frowned. "There's enough ugliness in this world. Why taint the kids with it?"

If this were simply a case of a single naive layman, misguided but faithful, we'd have one problem. But it's bigger than that, because the same clergymen who scoff at her theological ignorance practice the same de-manuring on grander scales. The whole world comes out sweet-smelling.

One fellow, glorious in multicolored robes and

perky collar, stood high in his pulpit on a glorious summer morning and got himself carried away with the whole thing. "God's in His heaven and all's right with the world," he smiled. Which would have been a dandy beginning had he gone on to say that God loves, despite the world's troubles, or something like that. But what he wound up saying was that the troubles are small, the difficulties blown out of proportion. It was really a beautiful world after all, with lilac and rosebuds, and trimmed hedges around the church property.

And I guess you could even stomach that romanticism, had it not been for the fact that just a few miles away, a city was being burned and looted by rioters.

Yes sir: the hay surely smelled sweet. If you happened to live out of earshot of the machine guns, that is. Had he been a little closer to the action, his nostrils would have been cluttered up with smoke from blazing buildings and burning flesh. But I guess he would have seen something beautiful in that, too. After all, God made fire first, didn't He?

My question is, who's confronting whom? Just when do those little kids get to hear that it's a troubled world, and that they have responsibilities in it? Who tells that preacher about violence and hate? Who acts to preserve the gospel's message of God-loves-man-and-we-love-too?

In professional church circles, the sad story of a woman-craving pastor is whispered from city to city. Most of my friends know about it by now. He's been caught in several adulterous situations, and he's broken up several marriages. He's a sick man, and I feel sorry for him. But the people who have dealt with him are sick too, and I have less sympathy for them.

This man's gone from church to church, following the same pattern.

He's been in serious trouble in several congregations. And each time, the church officers have met quietly and hushed up the whole thing, allowing him to "resign" and take another pulpit. In at least one instance, they gave him six months to relocate. Since he has a good bearing and excellent stature, he is an ideal candidate. And he has always managed to get a good spot.

But who stopped the cycle by calling in the church authorities and leading him toward psychiatric help? Who was brave enough to confront the church with its newest candidate for sinner-of-the-year? And how many families were harmed because of their "love" for the poor man?

If you're looking for good examples of confrontation-less activities, a likely place to start is with a pulpit committee.

In Protestant, Reformed-tradition circles, it's the pulpit committee that gets to act first. They hear a dozen or so candidates, sometimes on the sly, and they interview the ones they like. Then the list gets narrowed down, and finally they zero in on a top prospect. (You can usually tell in advance the kind of guy they're going to get; take the previous pastor and find his personality-antithesis, and you're pretty close.)

Now comes the final interview. He asks about salary and manse and car allowance, and they ask about number of children and whether he likes junior choirs. Who asks about the gospel? Presumably the Holy Spirit, that's who.

Now somewhere along the line, I'm sure that conscientious pastors ask responsible questions, and that concerned pulpit committees fire them right back at him. Only thing is, that hasn't happened where I've seen the committee at work. And the results are pathetic.

One young fellow went through a whole series of interviews in which they discussed everything from the color of his car to whether his wife wore glasses. They left out only a few simple topics. Like the fact that this was a suburban church on the borderline of a Negro community panting for equal-housing opportunities, and that this suburb itself was embroiled in a heated controversy that had torn the whole town asunder.

Did someone on that committee ask this man where he stood on some of these hot issues? Nope. Did he ferret out the real congregational concerns? Nope. Did he get hired? Yup.

And there he sits today, a bastion of reaction in the face of social illness, leading his congregation right smack into the face of — ignorance.

He had views, all right. He later spelled them out: "I think the Negro has to earn the right to move to the suburbs, like I did." And so forth. Seems he had seen dirty Negroes; he *knew* how they lived.

Now this particular congregation has denominational ties that, in theory, could have been used to prevent this kind of mis-match. There is a higher authority that theoretically offers guidance in these hiring situations. There is a functioning committee whose job it is to dig into these new relationships, and make certain that the right man gets in the right pulpit.

Did *it* ask those pertinent questions? Nope. Did *it* interview the man? Nope. Was *it* in favor of his being hired, by default? Yup.

So who's confronting whom?

Or is confrontation outdated? Do current circumstances change the picture, so that today's world requires something different?

Some tell me they do. Okay, so I'm a lousy shortstop and I can't play the outfield either. But I'm still on the team, and unless the coach has changed the rules, I think the old ones still apply.

I can't accept the argument that "this man has a ministry too," for instance. Sure he does, but what kind? And I have difficulty gulping down the argument that God can work through him as well as through more faithful pastors. Of course God can. If God's as big as I picture Him, He can accomplish His will in His own way, in His own time, through whomever He chooses.

But what does that have to do with *my* responsibility? Forget the "judge not" command here, too, because I'm not saying this reactionary pastor is doomed to perdition. What I am saying is that in response to the gospel, I am required to *do* something, to act. And God asks me to proclaim that gospel in the most responsible way I can. He asks me to confront the world with it. And to confront the world where I am — where He put me, if you prefer it that way.

So this man has a ministry; all right, let's find it, and see that nobody is hurt by it, at least. He's strong on holding little old ladies' hands? Let's make him a handholder. A handholder without par. But let's not allow him to take a job in a sensitive spot like this one, knowing full well that he's hardly aware of his surroundings. (In this case from real life, the saddest part of the story is that the previous pastor had made some real headway with the Christians in that congregation; actually, the new man was *behind them* in awareness.)

When I run into situations like this I grope around for something to say. And for several years I had to say little when they told me about another one of these confrontation-less affairs, because I was too stunned. I used to mutter something about "how sad" out of the corner of my mouth, and smile an embarrassed smile, and walk away.

But then I stumbled across a rather interesting question, and I've been having a fine time using it ever since. It goes like this:

HE: "Well, I guess we're stuck with old John out there. Poor John; you know, he's just incapable. He's just a burden on that congregation. It'll be good for them when he finally retires."

ME: "Well, what are you fellows going to do about it?"

HE: "Oh, I guess there's not much we can do, really. I talked with him the other day, and I sort of felt him out, asking him when he was going to hang up the robes and quit."

ME: *"Oh, just the way Jesus would have played it, huh?"*

It's fascinating to watch the response that this prodding little question gets. An eyebrow shoots upward, a lip curls in a brief moment of anger, and then settles down into a beatific smile.

HE: "Yeah, well, I guess I'd better be getting along now."

(Still there, Jesus? Hope you caught the exchange. I sure confronted him, didn't I?)

Once in a while, some of these fellows get together and get collectively worried about such failures. Their worry takes all sorts of forms. One of the most popular is called a meeting.

Chapter Three Non-Questions, Super-Questions and a Disease Called Verbitis

I REMEMBER A VERY FRUSTRATING CONVERSATION that took place just after a clergyman friend had returned from a consultation. He and his colleagues were studying the threat of automation and technology to society.

Now that's a worthy enough target for Christian concern (although whether it was worth bringing fifteen or twenty men one thousand miles to discuss is another question).

My friend came back happy. It was a "good" consultation, he said. A "successful" one.

"What were your conclusions?" I made the mistake of asking.

"Well . . . . " Long pause. Then finally, "We heard some speakers who really opened our eyes."

"And they concluded?"

"They concluded that the local church ought to recognize this impending threat and plan strategy for it."

"How?"

"What do you mean, how?"

"How do you suggest the local church go about 'recognizing this threat and planning strategy'?"

(Second long pause.)

"How do you suggest they go about this?"

"I don't know. We didn't get into that."

What bothers me is that this is probably a typical church consultation. You start with a big subject; you bring in experts from several allied disciplines; and you spend a day, or several days, listening to fact and opinion.

As a pragmatist, I have to ask a simple question: Why?

Why bother? The experts are all around us, the library shelves full of their findings on all sorts of "threats to society." The secular world is quite capable of isolating and defining those threats, it seems. I read about them on the columnists' page of my daily paper every evening. Every major magazine deals with them, some in remarkable depth. Higher education dwells on them year after year.

Automation and cybernetics, the popular twin threats of the moment, are good examples. There is deep, quality study being conducted all over this nation on that pair of latter-day devils. Sociologists have been warning about them for years. They talk of depersonalization, loss of individuality, the working-force balance. And they talk and write capably.

So my first question has to be, Why? Why should the church jump onto a consultation bandwagon, merely to reach a foregone conclusion? And why should it spend thousands of dollars in the process?

There's a second question, too. How do we separate fact from theory in all of this? We've been hearing for several years now that in a few short years 2 percent of the labor force (or 5, or 10, depending on the expert) will be able to produce all the goods and services needed by the rest of us. And there's a great big moral question here, so the pattern goes. What's to become of our traditional concept of working and earning? What do we do to make the other 98 percent of the potential labor force feel human? What happens to the old Protestant ethic of work to earn your bread and then eat it?

Those are interesting, and disturbing, moral questions — *if the prediction is accurate*. But the prediction has been seriously challenged by students of history, who cite similar threats to society made in the beginning of the industrial revolution. Some of those experts are saying that U.S. society, at least, has always managed to come up with enough consumer services to more than balance the employment deficit.

If there is serious doubt about the forecast, it seems doubly wasteful to spend church money, time, and energy "consulting" about it. But even those consultations would exude a little more validity if there were some conclusions to be reached.

Do we dare call "recognize and plan" a conclusion? How do you "recognize a threat," anyway? And how in the world can you expect a local parish to "plan strategy" for it?

Which brings us to the whole language pattern of the church consultation.

Say I'm a man of action. I'm dedicated enough. I'm concerned about the world around me. But I'm not an expert. So I put my pennies into the offering plate and ask for guidance; which direction should my Christian concern go? Where should I focus my worry this week?

While I'm waiting, fifteen grown men spend a few thousand dollars of those collective pennies and go bask in a sunny consultation. They hear the latest theories from the latest theorists. They talk. They listen. They make tape recordings, or take copious notes, or both. They mimeograph those speeches, and then they come back to me, Mr. Average Concerned Christian.

"Be aware of this," they say. "Recognize the implications; plan strategy to deal with it on a local level."

Great! First of all, I've been hearing about it for years. What do they have to add? Second, how valid are the predictions? Third, how do I recognize a threat? Fourth, how do I plan strategy?

I might just give up and go back to tossing in more pennies, out of total confusion.

Not that I don't want to hear about what's about to happen to my fellow man; yea, even my grandchildren.

I'm concerned about their world. But what I want to hear for my pennies is something with some meat on it.

And I want them to be honest with me. I know of one group of men who'd been studying this work-force reduction threat for more than a year. Then they heard another expert one night, who discounted the whole threat as just a repeat of historical fears. "Relax," he told them. "It just isn't going to happen. It's never happened, and the odds are overwhelming that it won't happen this time. You need men to build computers, too, and others to service them. And there are goods and services that haven't even been dreamed up yet. They will be. They always have been. The 98 percent will dream them up, plan them, and work at them. Your threat is a myth."

This expert had all the credentials of the others. And here he was, telling the church to think twice before it put so much money and effort into what could turn out to be a meaningless worry.

The church's reaction? You guessed it. They mimeographed his speech (in a very small quantity), and went right on planning for that poor unemployed 98 percent. The possible myth had already turned into reality, and it was too late to stop the consultation wheels from rolling on down dollar hill.

Three days later I heard a worrying churchman, a veteran of that speech and others, repeating the same 2 percent argument all over again, *as fact*. And the planners went on planning. They still are.

They're also still talking abstractly. I've been told by the clericalized experts recently to "behold the consequences," to "spot the implications," to "hasten the day," and to "grasp the opportunities."

Now I'm a practical man. And an anxious one. I'd sincerely like to get a handle on some of these problems of our times. But how in the world do I "hasten the day?" If astronomers can't alter the orbit of the moon, how am I supposed to speed the earth around the sun faster?

And how do I grasp an opportunity? By the tail? The mane? The middle syllable?

If I ever see an implication, how do I go about spotting it? With a paintbrush? Or will colored water do, if I flick it from my fingertips?

I'm not poking idle fun at these fellow concerned Christians. I'm asking, sincerely, what they want me to do. They've thoughtfully come up with something that's going to harm my brothers, God's creatures. And I am concerned about my brothers, God's creatures. But how do I express that concern? By beholding a consequence? I've never even seen one!

On the other hand, I *have* seen obvious ills in society. I have seen war, and racial strife, and poverty, and middle-class woes. I'd be happy to write my congressman about them again, or give more of my money for an organized lobby to drive for remedial legislation, or even stand in protest — putting my body on the line for my beliefs.

I'm willing to pile all the latest books on the subject in the back of my car, and take them over to the church, or to somebody's living room, so that we can dissect them, study them, and get a clearer picture of what those experts are telling us. I'm willing to take part in study groups that want to get into the action. I'm willing to talk on the subject, and to listen. I'm willing to act.

But I'm not willing to spot, hasten, behold or grasp anything I can't see or put my hands on. At heart, I'm just a plain old Doubting Edward. I gotta see it to act on it.

And if they can't point it out to me, then what are they doing? Where are they heading? For what purpose? With whose money?

I suspect that they're afflicted with a serious disease, one that I'll call verbitis, or inflamation of the verb. Furthermore, I think it's become pandemic.

Another august committee spent a lot of time wrestling with another of America's big problems. Their recommendation: that the church "foster real confrontation" and that individual Christians "face their own general status."

Now I'm really confused. Which way do I turn to "face my own general status?" Or do I pivot toward a looking glass? "Mirror, mirror on the wall, who's the fairest general status of them all?"

Nor is "supporting a principle" any more helpful.

Now I can support a growing boy, maybe, or a rocking chair. But a principle . . . ? And I absolutely refuse to "foster" anything, simply because I've no idea what that one means at all. Webster says it means to cherish, sustain or promote. Okay, I'll promote a real confrontation — provided somebody tells me how.

Tell me how and I'm off and running. Give me a verb I can act on. Tell me to move out, to get off my seat, to petition Congress, to fire my pastor, to fire up my church officers with rhetoric, to picket my local food store — tell me to do something. Anything.

If they don't, I'm going to demand that one of these groups "create an atmosphere," and I'm going to demand that in self-defense. That'll fix them.

Knowing the way church groups operate, though, I guess they'd probably come right back at me with a new committee to study atmosphere creation.

I remember one such group, formed to study something called "feedback." Now the mission was plain when the group was organized. They wanted to put something out, and they wanted feedback on it — in other words, how were people taking it? It was a standard old case of the stock old Madison Avenue line that has a thousand-and-one variations:

— Let's run it up the flagpole and see who salutes.

— Let's dress it in a miniskirt and see who looks.

— Et cetera.

What they wanted to know, simply, was how people felt about it, this new thing they were launching.

Simple enough, eh?

Not a chance. Not the way the church handles it.

The committee opened, naturally, with prayer. "Open our eyes, Lord, and give us Thy guidance."

As it turned out, they *should* have prayed, "Be patient, Lord, because we're closing our eyes for a while now . . . . "

There was no formal agenda, so naturally they had to start working on one. That took the better part of one full meeting day. And then the serious business.

"Well," ventured a daring Christian, "we're here to devise ways to get better feedback on this."

Dead silence.

The chairman spoke: "Maybe we'd better look at some of the implications of this word 'feedback.' "

(That was a key right there. Ever try looking an implication in the face?)

"What do we *mean*, feedback?"

Now somewhere along the line we'd lost something. We started by knowing full well what we meant by the word feedback. We sat down around that big table with a pretty clear idea of what we were there for. Now we had regressed. Now we didn't even know what the word meant.

The chairman's question led to a blackboard diagram of possible feedback patterns. That led to an "overall chart" on the whole question, and *that* led into another scheduled meeting.

Two meetings later, we still hadn't defined the word feedback. The chairman must have felt some real progress, though, because he kept thanking the committee for "really getting into the meat of this problem."

Then finally it came. A breakthrough. We put a definition into words. Well, not exactly a firmed-up definition, but at least a draft of one.

We had to kick that draft around for quite some time, of course. And eventually we kicked it upstairs, to the larger committee. They murmured an assent and sent it back. Now we had a working definition.

Now we could get on with the business of devising feedback methods, right? Wrong.

First came another vital preliminary step — one we would have missed entirely had not one of our more thoughtful members raised the subject. It came just after the chairman acknowledged that we'd acquired a working definition.

"What do we mean, working definition?" asked our thoughtful colleague.

I was tempted, but I said it only to myself: "What do we *mean*, mean?"

"What do we *mean* . . . " is a non-question that ought to be awarded a grand prize for uselessness. "What does it *mean* to be a Christian in today's world?" Or "What does it *mean* to serve as an usher in church?" Or "What do we really *mean* by the term 'servant ministry'?"

The epitome of it all is reached along about the time a committee on urban ministry asks, "What does it *mean* to minister?"

That's a nice question, and a perfectly valid one. Except for several things:

(1) It's been asked, and answered, a zillion times.
(2) Anybody who hasn't caught up with the answer is probably in the wrong business.
(3) While the non-question is being asked once more, the urban ministry dilemma goes unsolved and unworked on.

The non-question isn't the supreme example, though. The super-question goes it one better. It goes like this:

"Can a student really be a person in today's big multiuniversity?" Or "Can a Christian really live a life of service in a secular world come of age?"

If that's a real, down-to-earth question, the answer is an obvious and ringing "Yes, of course!" If, on the other hand, it's a rhetoric question, I'm tempted to wonder what we're doing playing around with rhetoric at a time like this.

I know the church isn't General Motors, but can't you just see those non-questions and super-questions being asked in a GM divisional meeting?

"Well, we've got a new design for the 1996 Chevy, and our purpose here today is to pick a basic theme for an ad campaign."

"What do we *mean,* basic theme?"

"Yeah, boss, and what do we *mean*, ad campaign?"

Then the topper: "Boss, I think there's a real implication for the whole motoring world in all of this, and I think we'd better deal with it right away. Can a Chevy really be a means of transportation in an age of wall-to-wall television?"

Well, what's good for General Motors has got to be good for the church of Jesus Christ, right?

(Hang on, Jesus, we're getting down to basics now, and just as soon as we get some of these preliminary questions out of the way we'll get right on it . . . .)

Chapter Four The Eleven-Minute Hour

THE SHINING BRICK CHURCH, SPRAWLING OVER A full city block, was the neighborhood's most attractive building. It had a hundred million rooms for study, four sanctuaries, a room for brides, another one for bridegrooms, one for grieving families at funerals, six kitchens, an arena big enough to seat a World Series crowd, and at least a dozen ladies' parlors. I didn't really look that closely (being limited to a one-day visit), but it probably had somewhere a room where the new couples could consummate their marriage, too.

I was being given my Sunday morning tour just before I had to address a church-school group on the subject of 20th-century church education. My audience was to be parents of college children, who had their own Sunday school class.

I was scheduled for 9:30 A.M., and since it was now 9:28 I exhibited a little nervousness for the time. "Don't worry," said my tour guide. "They're having coffee first anyhow."

We got to the room, finally, and wedged our way past a couple dozen couples. We had our coffee. We were granted a few introductions, to the president of the class, the first vice president, the secretary, the business manager, and probably the director of public relations.

And this is an honest chronology of what happened:

9:48 A.M. — The president gavelled for order, and people started drifting back to the rear of the room to deposit their empty coffee cups.

9:59 A.M. — The group was called to order with prayer.

10:02 A.M. — The business meeting was formally opened.

10:12 A.M. — The business meeting was formally closed.

10:13 A.M. — They started singing hymns.

10:18 A.M. — They finished singing hymns.

10:19 A.M. — They introduced me.

I was speaking to a Sunday school group that had a "one-hour" class, and they'd left me eleven minutes! Because I was from out of town — *way* out of town — and was going to get on an airplane and leave for home that afternoon, I thought I was relatively safe in tossing out my text and dwelling, instead, on the futility of this "learning" situation. I did. For nearly six whole minutes, before a clanging bell warned us that the period would be over in five minutes.

At the clang, half the class stirred to leave. Seems they had some other church obligations, and had to get a head start on their colleagues. For them it was a six-minute hour.

Now this congregation (no, it's not the one you're thinking of) probably carried things to extremes. But I have to wonder just how extreme. Certainly the sixty-minute Sunday school hour is the shortest hour since Freud bought his first couch. I've yet to see one that lasted more than fifty minutes, tops, and most I've watched put about forty minutes into actual study. If you call it that.

And let's not get too deeply into that "study," because that's worth a few books of its own.

Suffice to say that the typical Sunday school is taught by teachers who don't want to teach, attended by students who'd rather not be there, sent by parents who don't know why they insist on kids attending, and watched over by a pastor who knows better, but who doesn't know what to do next.

In too many congregations, a teacher is a person who couldn't say No fast enough.

(So we get the slow thinkers for teachers!)

And in all too many churches, Sunday school is perhaps the most confusing of all congregational activities.

Organized religion's answer to this has been typically bureaucratic, symbolized by a 1966 Atlantic City, N. J., incident. It was in that resort town that Christian educators met to swap ideas and information. In the course of the meeting, a local wire-service reporter sensed a story; church education was changing drastically, and he wanted to know why. He interviewed half a dozen experts, and came up with a feature that told the story well. In essence, it said that times had changed, and so church education had to take on new forms.

But he made the mistake of getting too realistic.

"Sunday school is a Sunday morning circus," said an enthusiastic educator. And the writer pounced on that as a good opening quote.

The repercussions were heard all the way to Palo Alto. They came not from teachers and students, but from local church pros. Here we are working our heads off, they said in effect, and here is our national staff caricaturing our efforts.

Now they had an apparent point, to be sure. But not as much of a point as the mere retelling suggests. First of all, they *knew*, as did the Atlantic City conferees, that new forms were needed fast. They themselves had been pleading for the new forms. They themselves had willingly accepted the changes. They just didn't want it said aloud.

So here were scores of educators (among thousands in this one denomination) pleading for radical change, accepting the radical ideas — but protesting angrily because someone finally put into words what had been said hundreds of times before in theological jargon.

The result was that a retraction was issued; Sunday school as we know it was "in" again. Somehow, incredibly, the radical changes would take effect — without ever having displaced anything!

Worse yet: the phrase "Sunday school" as used by the reporter was roundly denounced at the Atlantic City meetings. The experts wanted "Sunday church school" used. One said, "That one phrase in the story has set our program back ten years."

Ho-hum.

What I'm trying to illustrate is that the institutional church's response to an obvious need has been to suggest radical changes. But no one seems to have guts enough to condemn the failures. And Sunday school goes on. And on.

It just might be, too, that the system *cannot accept* radical changes. Certainly it cannot accept anything that threatens the form of the structure itself. The system is there, *ergo*, anything new must fit the system.

One educator came back from an extensive tour with a simplified description of one problem, and a simplified response. It went like this:

Most teachers, he thought, had precious little scriptural background, a meager knowledge of church history, and no inkling of what theology was. Not surprisingly, he found teachers who grossly misquoted the Bible, who had distorted views of the church, who were clinging to a twisted theology. He saw the need for a simplified course in Christianity, and he had an idea. Why not produce an inexpensive loose-leaf notebook, filled with easily read sections on basic questions? He wanted four or five pages telling — simply — what the Old Testament was all about; the prophets' concerns, the concept of Judaic law, etc. Then another few pages on the life of Christ, and so on.

His idea was greeted warmly by his colleagues, who had seen the same need. But it was rejected by his bureaucracy because "*We cannot publish something that cheap-looking*." A few callous souls pointed out that this bureaucracy was geared to high-profit publishing, and that something as pedestrian as a loose-leaf notebook just didn't fit as did, say, a hard-cover book. And one particularly profit-conscious cleric went even one step further: "If we print stuff like that, you'll be out of a job," he intoned. "We just can't support a staff of church-school editors on those kind of profits."

I'd supposed, naively, that this agency existed to serve the church.

But if the national church cannot supply the leadership, and lacks the courage to write off the failures, where next?

Where next indeed. Certainly the Sunday schools have produced a generation of Biblical illiterates. Certainly (witness backlash to the racial revolution, the foreign policy rebellion) they've not supplied great numbers of concerned Christians, reading newspapers in one hand and Bibles in the other.

Certainly attendance is down drastically, and interest is sagging, if not skidding to all-time lows. But the point is that we cling to the Sunday school — a 300 year-old institution — as if it were Pauline. And the national church structure tries valiantly to produce (high-profit?) curricula that will perpetuate the failures.

Once in a while new things happen. But when they do, they are invariably set into motion by gung-ho individuals who then have to weather a storm of status-quo protest. A man I know, pastor of an upper-middle-class congregation, had the nerve to scrap the failures and start anew. He gathered up his local talent, of which there was plenty, and devised his own curriculum. He made innovations to insure that there'd be better attendance. He used released-time from public schools for his classroom hours. He had local teachers at work, as well as a child psychologist and other home-grown experts. He didn't solve all the problems, but he did get rid of most of the dead-wood concepts.

And while he was busily at work getting something going, a national-staff expert was roundly condeming his efforts (in private) as "bad church education." The staff man, of course, insisted that he knew what "good" church education was. It would have been unfair of me to ask him why he didn't pass on a few of his cherished secrets.

The staffer's condemnation illustrates a more important point: Is it not in the interest of a more faithful church to raise the "good/bad education" theories so that all can benefit? This man spent a week or so cornering colleagues, poking fun at his counterpart in the local church. But he never did say what was "bad" about the plan, and he never did contact the local man to pass on his suggestions.

I have to suspect, of course, that he was just plain envious of a man who'd done something differently. Which is a downright second-rate road to progress.

But let's suppose the local effort was *bad* education, and that our national hero had all the answers. Is there not enough honesty in this church to deal with controversy where people can see it?

No, there isn't.

A misguided honesty pervades the whole mixed-up church school business, just as it does the church. Honesty is there, of course. But it's covered with institutional layers of fatty protocol, and it requires major surgery to dig it out.

Honesty, and just plain competence, are hidden equally well on the local level.

We've all known teachers who reluctantly accepted the job, then botched it with the recklessness that only complete incompetence can supply. Of course the even sadder example is the teacher who plods on from week to week, getting across practically zilch to a captive audience and fooling unsuspecting parents as well. I'd want to guess that her name is legion, that *most* parents have little idea of just what it is that transpires inside those noise partitions — what passes for "education."

The sweet little old lady is the most insidious of all, because no pastor in his right mind would pick on a sweet little old lady, and she's "so certain" that her kids in school are "so basically good" and that she's producing nice, clean Christian adults.

Watch her, though. She's running things. And the church isn't doing anything about it.

"They're really wonderful children," she gushes. And who's going to argue with that?

Curriculum choice is another weak spot. And here, too, the gushy little lady with the twisted theology holds forth. It is she who's likely to suggest that the nasty (i.e., serious) stuff is all right for older youngsters, but that the "sweet little ones" ought to be getting nice (i.e., meaningless) materials to use. And in a lot of otherwise mission-minded churches, you'll find the awfulest conglomeration of curriculum entrees.

I've seen — you've seen, we've all seen — churches where a fairly liberal curriculum was mixed with heady conservative stuff in indiscriminate batches. Where youngsters were spoon-fed from David C. Cook and then tossed a sophisticated dose of Seabury Press, or vice versa. And we wonder why we have rebellious kids?

They'll also rebel when a Sunday school can't keep up with their level of development (and I dare you to name four that can). We've seen kids who jump into solid-state physics in high school, then get pushed into a Sunday morning experience where they're asked to take Jonah, whole, and don't ask questions. Or study Moses. Again.

When I used to speak on the subject, I illustrated that point with the gag about the two kindergarten kids at recess arguing about rocket launching. One insists that the G-forces can be overcome someday artificially, and the other battles back in favor of natural law. Then the bell rings, and the first kid turns and gripes, "Okay, it's time to go back in and string those beads again!"

(Hang on, Jesus. We're going to inspire those kids with two new Bible verses and a flannel graph.)

Chapter Five

It's Only Money

I'D LIKE TO KNOW HOW MUCH MONEY IT COSTS TO:

— Hold a national consultation. The fruitless kind.
— Set up a committee to study ways "in which we relate to . . . . " (Fill in your own ending.)
— Keep people on church payrolls who shouldn't be there.
— Proclaim officially about things we know little about.

I already know how much money it costs to do other needless things in the church, and brother, we go first-class.

I know that one big prestigious church recently

agreed to pay $2400 a month — base fee — to a public relations agency.

I know that a study of teaching effectiveness cost one denomination more than $30,000, and probably close to $40,000. And it wasn't used.

I know that one denomination paid about $10,000 to make a movie that sits in a vault somewhere because it was too controversial to show.

I know of one $10,000-a-year man, an incompetent man, who was kept on the payroll of a national church headquarters for a year so that he could find "just the right kind" of job.

And I know that one denomination shelled out $8 million to build a national church and center — at the very time that poverty became a recognized social evil.

The point is, money is scarce in church hierarchies, but there has been little belt-tightening yet. Instead, we keep pitching for more money, "just to continue the things we're doing now." And there are times when the pitch gets a little embarrassing to make.

I was tapped a few years ago to go on a four-man speech-making tour of North Dakota. Its purpose was to inspire churchmen to raise the ante. We spent a week or so combing the North Dakota flatlands for tiny little churches, whose memberships seldom topped 200 souls, and bringing the message of service to assembled groups of maybe 15 to 20 people. Here, pastors were paid $5,000 plus car allowance to serve three congregations. Here, members were battling a hostile land and an increasing threat of banking/farming cartels. Here, tiny churches with rotting clapboard dwindled into ill-kept monuments. Urban riots and even ghettos were as foreign as Punjab poverty. And into this setting we marched, with our salary checks held high, pleading for understanding — and more cash.

At one meeting I was surrounded by men in Sears-catalog suits and women in Montgomery-Ward gingham, who'd put something resembling a casserole together. We all gave our little speeches, and the foreign missions man stressed that the government of India was "taking over" the hospital business there, relegating the ill-equipped Christian hospitals to a poor second place. "The government hospitals are well-staffed and well-equipped," he said. "With such good facilities and service, nobody wants to go to the Christian hospital anymore."

And then he spent the next five minutes pleading for money, so that the Christian hospital could be maintained. Not for better medical care. For the simple *de facto* reason that they were there first.

National bureaucracies, of course, are the epitome of big-spending institutions. The payrolls run into the millions, and you'd be surprised at how little you get for it. I've known national-agency bureaucrats who've been on the scene for a decade and more, running all over the country, but whose jobs defy description simply because they don't do anything. And there are a lot of them.

One fellow stands out. Every other day, it seems, he was heading for another trouble spot. "Gotta run," he'd breathe heavily to his secretary. "You can catch me at the airport in Jackson, Mississippi, if you need me. Call you first thing in the morning." Then, topcoat in hand and two-suiter in tow, he'd head for the nearest cab. "Gotta get down there," he'd say, "because there's a whole mess of trouble down there."

And off he'd go, to meet with a few church types and discuss the problems brought on by the local government's refusal to distribute food stamps to its poor. Sounds big-time, huh? Don't believe it. This fellow had no control over the situation, no program to recommend, no ideas for potential solutions, nothing to offer except talk. But he'd be there, in person, with bells on. Bells paid for by little kids who'd saved their pennies for the church.

Figure out the cost of a New York-Mississippi trip by air and rented car, then add in hotels (no flea bags for our big-timer), meals, tips, a drink or two to keep him happy, and incidentals. This man had a travel budget of about $7,000 a year. And no one I knew could tell me what he did for a living!

And in my own denomination, the annual meeting has drawn scores of such characters, all on good-sized expense accounts. You may see them floating around the hotels, downing $7.50 steaks and $1.50 martinis, and holding dozens of "meetings" in $65 a day suites. No, you aren't able to find out what they are doing, either.

Things ease up a bit in the summer, though. A lot of church bureaucrats manage to find two or three summer events they can wedge into vacation schedules, and it turns out that they and their families are gone for up to three months — expenses paid.

The dollars go out, with such little return, primarily because there is no effective control. And precious little real leadership. A national agency is a power to itself, often "governed" by an elected board whose members are virtually named by agency staff employees. The result is practically no government whatsoever. And what comes out might best be described as prayerful chaos.

If the Holy Spirit runs things, it's a good thing He does. Because nobody else does.

I know a fellow who took European vacations every summer — at church expense. I know a guy who shuffled thousands of papers all year long, but who couldn't tell you what his job was. I know a woman who once spent almost an hour trying to define her committee's assignment — and failed.

And I know that these people are not a tiny minority.

All this, of course, is done *without* malice aforethought. I want to stress that, because I'm not calling these people thieves. I am saying that they don't really know *what* to do, and have little competence to start with. And so bureaucratic paper-shuffling and vacation-scheduling takes priority. The control lid is off, and abuses become easy.

In most institutions, some clear line of control (and judgment) is defined for all to see. You know who the boss is, and where he gets his rules. And you have a pretty good idea of what your neighbor does. In the church institution, all the lines are blurred by a super Pill that prevents the church from ever being impregnated by too much efficiency. The Pill is called theology, or faith, or hope, or maybe all three. I call it *status-quo-ism*.

But what else can you expect? You take a man

whose training has been in pastoral work, and give him a national job because he couldn't quite hack it outside. Overnight he's an instant expert. Then you give him a good salary, a generous travel allowance, and an ambiguous assignment. And let Parkinson's Law set in. As I said, what else can you expect ? (Just to make it worse, add the fact that nobody gets fired. After a while you have an entrenched bureaucrat who can justify his existence merely by being there. The job is an end to itself.)

In my own denomination, an annual General Assembly supposedly oversees all these operations. But that five-day affair is so tightly fitted with arranged-for business that a real gripe can hardly be made. I've often wondered what would happen if elected representatives to that Assembly were to ask just one question of every bureaucrat they met: "What are you doing here?"

If a national church structure wants to spend $25,000 on an exhibit for that Assembly, nobody has the opportunity to ask why. If it wants to send 250 men and women to that meeting, as a sort of mid-year reward, nobody would dare ask why.

Not that asking would help much. I've heard so many guys tell me that their job was to "get plugged into" the next guy, that I'm tempted to turn on the juice. That's part of the phraseology of the decade, you know:

"What do you do?"

"I'm plugged into those three coordinators."

"What do they do?"

"They sensitize the church."

"How?"

"By getting plugged into all available sources."

"And you?"

"I quarterback their efforts."

Just what every good ball club needs: a sensitized, plugged-in quarterback.

Does all that plugging-in result in creative thought? New ideas? Forget it. The plug may be there, but the voltage wouldn't handle a Lionel train, much less a yard full of over-burdened freight cars. Sometimes the simplest of ideas gets drowned out by the noise of solemn bureaucracies. One I won't forget for a while:

A repairman for an electric typewriter company came into the office, made his repair, charged us $12.50 for a service call, and asked directions to another office. "Do you charge them all $12.50?" our enterprising office manager asked. "Yes; each call is billed $12.50," he replied. And in a brilliant flash of economy, the woman manager tracked down the bureaucrat in charge.

"It won't save that much, maybe a thousand or two a year," she said. "But we could get the whole building to cooperate on calls for typewriter repairs, and we'd only be billed a single $12.50—even though the man has to make nine stops while he's here."

Was she rewarded with a trip to Bermuda for two? A $100 incentive bonus? A smile and congratulations? Nope. Instead she heard her boss say simply that "we don't want to get into that." She was sent back to her office, to sin no more.

(Sometimes I wonder, Lord.)

Chapter Six Some Ways Out

IT'S WORTH REPEATING: ONE OF BUREAUCRACY'S biggest difficulties is that it has no checks and balances. The church agency that (to all intents) names its own governing board really has no one to look after it. The bureaucrat on a junket isn't going to challenge his colleague's plans for the summer.

Obviously, we need to set up a series of checks and balances to keep the institution in rein. As churchmen, we owe it to ourselves. As Christians, we may owe it to our God.

But that kind of drastic reform won't be suggested by the bureaucracy itself. It cannot validly ask that question; it simply has too much at stake. After awhile the maintenance syndrome has set in; the institution exists to maintain itself, and no insider can raise the question of its very existence and get an honest answer.

As a friend once told me, "The trouble with introspection is that when you step outside yourself and ring the doorbell, nobody's left to answer it."

Logically, the question is going to have to be raised from outside. But who's going to ask it, with what authority? It cannot be the elected board member — he's an insider, too. It cannot be the run-of-the-pulpit pastor, since the cards are all stacked against him. Few outside "consultants" are going to risk alienating their clients with such probing questions, and I seriously doubt if they'd get much of an answer anyhow.

It's left in our hands, then.

And here we have a clear choice. We can ignore it — obviously we've been doing just that for a long time. We can rationalize it ("Christ said He'd build His church, and this is still part of the building process"). We can justify it ("There always have been abuses, and there always will be. And in the main, a few abuses aren't really so bad. After all, look at big government"). Or we can see our responsibility to do something about it.

If we see a clear mandate to act, we have some circumstances on our side. This is a masochistic age for the mainline Protestant church; she's primed and ready to be told of her ills. She's in serious financial trouble. She's on the verge of a split over social issues. She's hurting, and she knows it. What better time than now to drive the point home?

Of all the symptoms, the financial plight is perhaps most existential. Nothing talks like money does, and I've recently heard bureaucrats beginning to squirm under the dollar press. This, then, is one very solid clue. If we can tie our reform to dollar bills, chances are we'll be heard — and listened to.

And in one sense, this is an automatic reforming process. Fewer dollars mean fewer jobs, and what follows is bound to be a housecleaning. Some of the fat just has to be trimmed off, because the input won't support it all. Some of the bigger inequities are going to die out for lack of cash. A few of those jobless types are going to have to go out and work for a living now. Some others are going to have to find new ways to justify their existence.

But if we let it stop there, we've abandoned our role as responsible reformers.

That kind of cause-and-effect reformation can last only as long as the dollar drain. Let giving pick up, and new boon-doggles will be invented as fast as the payroll department can keep up with them. Without new checks and balances, nothing lies in their path.

What we need is a deterrent, and an effective one. What we need is responsible cynicism, with maybe a touch of iconoclasm tossed in.

We will get it when the individual sees his responsibility to act. We'll have it when ordinary people move. What's missing is just a mode of operation. Here's one super-suggestion:

(Brilliant, huh, Lord? Set them up with logic, and then sock them with the idea I had in mind way back on Page 1. I'd like a special place at your right hand for that little maneuver.)

Let individuals act in their own circumstances, keeping in mind their duty to *question and challenge everything*. Let them keep one hand on their purse strings while the other hand thrusts an accusing forefinger at the whole establishment. Let them remember as they go about their nasty chores that an offense is the best defense. Let them probe and question, demand and insist, plead and pry. Let them pick their spots. Let them push and shove. Let them make their mistakes. But above all, *let them act*.

Painful? You bet. But what surgery can be accomplished without an incision? And cutting does hurt, even if the patient knows it's for his own good.

You and I can set up some painful surgery *where we are*, on the local level. We can do it by insisting that a big-business church act businesslike. Out of that should come controls that will put the bureaucracy in perspective.

That'll take care of the big institution. Now how about the local church, where we live? I have another theory:

(I did it again, Lord. Came up with another brilliant answer. I hope you were right when you said there were many mansions, because I plan to live in all of them before I'm through.)

The emphasis in my local church is on reconciliation, on healing. And that's good. Nobody wants to argue with that. But there is a time for splitting, too. There is a time to tear things asunder. There is a time when money-changers have to be tossed out on their bags of gold, when rightful anger *belongs*. Trouble is, anger seems to have no place in this super-healing atmosphere of ours.

I'm not talking about blasting the poor naive churchman who's confused, and who's looking for solace. I'm talking about the "churchman" who's downright *hostile* to the gospel. I know there's a piece of Scripture that says "Come unto me . . . . " But I also know there are other things scriptural, too. Like the segment in Hebrews that talks about laboring outside the camp — outside accepted society, if you will — and draws parallels between the "outside" Christian and the Christ who died outside His city.

Here, it seems to me, is a clear challenge for Christians of any age. The task is to be willing to accept social criticism. The test is to be willing to work at unpopular causes, things society doesn't buy readily. Things like lone-wolfing it in an acculturated church, for example. That manicured and irrelevant church on the corner is as much a part of "acceptable" society as is Bob Hope's Christmas show. And it's that society we have to be willing to shun, if necessary, in the interest of being faithful.

I think those things are worth getting angry over. Angry with justifications. (Jesus, after all, warns against *unjustified* anger. He says in Matthew's Gospel, "Whosoever is angry with his brother *without a cause* . . .").

Scripture also warns us to look out — because trouble is coming — when people speak well of us. That seems to be a long-forgotten warning. Today's churches seem too often to be battling each other for the privilege of having all men speak well of them. I remember a local Lutheran congregation whose pastor tried to instill a social conscience. He was told at a public meeting, "Why must we be the only church around here that's stirring up trouble?" I would have paraphrased it, "Why are we the only church around here that's trying to be faithful?"

When a congregation becomes a neighborhood social institution, offering trimmed lawns and hedges and a popular but meaningless Sunday message, I think it's time we recognized that congregation for exactly what it has become — a part of our American culture, little more. And just once I'd like to see the challenge raised.

That Lutheran pastor, for example, knows that he must protect his job. He has three kids to raise, and this pastoring business is his profession and his livelihood. I can't deny him that. He also knows that despite protestations to the contrary, a pastor is judged by the numbers. A man who goes into a 500-member church and increases its membership to 700 has done a good job.

A man going into a 200-member declining congregation who maintains that level has also been "successful." Of course those very numbers might indicate his *failure*. But try explaining *that* to a denominational headquarters or a prospective employer!

It's understandable, then, that my Lutheran friend would try to promote healing within his congregation. And it's theologically understandable, too, that he'd be in favor of reconciling those disparate elements in his membership. After all, what's as Christian as unity? But if his bag is reconciliation, then who does the confronting?

I contend that a good portion of his people were brought into the church under false pretenses. They promised nothing, understood little, were looking for a quiet country-club atmosphere. How do I know? Because they tell me so! They admit it. And many of these people are the ones who are resentful of the gospel and its implications. Then again, why shouldn't they be? They certainly had nothing like that in mind when they joined up, did they?

Okay, taking them in under those circumstances is one thing. But I can't see why we then have to dilute the gospel — or ignore it altogether — merely because those people comprise a portion of our church membership. You want to spend time "healing" a congregation with those elements? You want to try to "reconcile" them to others who've accepted the imperatives of the gospel, or who are sincerely trying to? I think you're wasting your time. And I think you're being unfaithful in the process.

I am not talking here about those honest conservatives to whom the social implications of the gospel are somehow less than valid. I think they're misguided, yes. I cannot agree when they see a "difference" between social action and "more meaningful" things, such as evangelism. I think the two are inseparable. I don't agree that Jesus may have had humanity in mind, but that He really came to do more important things. I think He was talking about one single problem — man's alienation. But I can understand what those self-styled conservatives are saying, and I won't fight them.

I cannot understand what the no-membership member has to say about all this. He wants his quiet Sunday morning atmosphere, maybe for cultural reasons. He respects the "preacher" as a holy guy who doesn't sin. He admits we have a "colored" problem, a poverty problem, a war problem. But he doesn't see where church membership has anything to do with those problems — either corporately or individually. To him, church is a piece of Americana. He's the fellow who responds to the drive-in movie's plea to "have faith." Faith in what? He tingles, maybe, when somebody sings "You'll Never Walk Alone." He accepts the banality of the public service ad, "Go to the church of your choice this week." But he'd have trouble with "Live your faith — Light the world." He is hostile to the message that Jesus proclaimed, the message of individual responsibility for my brother's need — caring for him even above self. He's openly in disagreement with all of that. And he's sitting there in that pew on Sunday morning, soaking up the atmosphere.

And you want me to water down Jesus' message to make him happy? Now that I've taken him in under false pretenses, you want me to change the rules of the game? I think that'd be spinning my wheels.

And once — just once — I'd like to see somebody challenge this guy.

On the following pages, I've outlined some simple suggestions for challenge, for change. Somewhere in those pages I hope you can find your own thing.

Chapter Seven

. . . Well, What Do You Suggest?

TO START WITH, DO NOT FORM A COMMITTEE TO study ways in which this little book can be studied. In fact, you might not even want to share it with a church group. The quickest way to inundate the ideas on these pages would be to drop them into the creaky old institutional machinery. You can picture it now: "We'll open with a panel and some reactors, then we'll break up into buzz groups, and then we'll come back together again for our final question of the night, 'Where do we go from here?' "

Poof. End of an idea. The institution wins again. Committees kill more ideas than they generate, by a ratio of five to one. (The Richter Survey [January 1969] indicates that the figure is actually closer to six to one in some areas of the country, notably the northwest. Based on a scientifically accurate sampling of four million committees and a little over nineteen ideas.)

What do we start with, then? I guess honesty is the best word. A plain, honest look at what we've got, and a simple honest attempt at changing it. Genuine reform is going to come from people, from you and me, and not from the bureaucracy that needs reforming. The one question that institution can never answer objectively is this: "Is this institution necessary?" It's the individual, not the group, that counts here. For that reason, we're going to have to start reformation where we are. And let's not even tell the institution about it, okay? Let's keep it our little secret.

Getting an honest start, though, is going to mean fighting off the institution's inherent opposition. It'll take many forms, and we might as well face it now. We'll hear several big counter-arguments, all designed to Stop the Movement Before It Starts. They bear watching, because they're insidious counter-arguments, and they'll sneak up on us fast. Here's one:

Abolish the institution, they'll say, and you're only going to have to devise another one to take its place.

This presupposes, of course, that we somehow *can* abolish the institution: that all we need to do is start talking reform and right away the structure has died. If we're going to be honest about that one, let's start by admitting that our efforts aren't going to turn the old girl around. We may make her take off a few pounds, and we may even get her to stick to a diet for awhile. And if we get really lucky, maybe she'll make some New Year's resolutions.

But she's going to be around long after we've gone, and we all know that. Let's worry about the "new" structure when the time comes, okay? Worrying about our substitute institution is just another way of replacing action with words.

And some action is preferable to none, as long as it's in the right direction. Let's start walking that honest road now, even if we have to content ourselves with a step or two. Let's not plan strategy for a road that leads we know not where. The old girl's clique would have us delay even a single step down that road until we can come up with a master plan, which makes about as much sense as refusing to amputate a gangrenous leg because we haven't yet developed an artificial limb.

Maybe we'll give her a transplanted heart (in time). And that's just fine, a worthy goal. But let's not settle for a face-lifting.

Another argument is based on that word strategy, which these days gets a popular modifying phrase, "long-range." "What's most strategic for our time?" is the way you'll hear it said when you suggest change.

What's most strategic is movement. A step, even a single one. What's most horrifying is that step one is going to be nipped in the kneecap because we're sitting here planning step ninety-three.

Suggested step one, I repeat, is for us to adopt the word honesty as our guideline. Honestly, now: where should our standard lie? With the church? With tradition? With scripture? Or with God? The very first question we can ask of ourselves is whether our action is faithful to God. It may be the only question we ever have to ask.

So let's start by asking it. How would Jesus have played it? What does He want me to do here, now?

Step two? Take a moment out to read a couple of those New Testament parables — the ones about the mustard seed, and the leaven. Scholars tell me they say something about God's being responsible for success, and about our responsibility for work. In other words, it's our job to work and it's God's job to decide just how effective we'll be. He'll take care of the results.

I'm not saying we shouldn't be realistic, or even pragmatic. I am saying that the long-range strategy committee will kill you cold before you can drop the mustard seed or the leaven. They'll do it with integrity, of course, and with sincerity. But that's not enough. Even Peanuts recognizes that sincerity falls short.

You'll also hear people say that you're oversimplifying the problem, or that you're way out on one side of the argument, and that someone else is way over on the other side, and that the truth probably lies somewhere in between. A good old mature judgment? Nope, just another popular blockade. Of course you've simplified the problem. How else do you deal with complexities but to break them down into not-so-complex segments? But *over*simplifying?

I'll tell you a secret: that's a word that means you're probably on the right track. Give me a guy who oversimplifies any day. He's probably getting the problem down to manageable size, anyhow.

And that "somewhere in between" truth could be

one of the biggest myths we've dealt with yet. Certainly it's the easiest way out of controversy. The Black Power men suggest radical steps in one direction, and the white bigot says "never," and the armchair apathy expert sits back, lights his pipe and exclaims in wise old tones, "The truth probably lies somewhere in between." Was Jesus far out on one side of the argument, or was He studiously lighting that pipe? Half the world starves, the other half diets, and our absurd apathy aficionado says the truth is in the middle. A wealthy congregation that hasn't done zilch to help its proverty-stricken neighbors decides to buy yet another sanctuary organ for $100,000, and our wise old man gets into the debate by saying that maybe a $50,000 organ and $50,000 worth of mission would make a good compromise.

Sometimes, dear reader friend, the truth is far, far out. Don't be stopped by those who would suggest a middle road. Certainly not on tactics as plainly evident as these:

(1) *Let's insist that the official language of our institution be English.*

Down with jargon like this, which recently appeared in a widely circulated strategy handbook: "As the church shapes itself for contact, involvement, and dialogue at the places where men do their work, it witnesses to its faith that Christ is governing, creating, redeeming and judging, as living Lord in the structures, processes, institutions, communities, and events of the metropolis."

(Suggested translation: "When the church *gets with it* in the city, where things are happening, it reflects Christ's love.")

Now we'll all admit that English can be a pretty complicated language. There are confusing words, and misused ones. Probably half the population says "who" instead of "whom," and says "meticulous" when it means "careful," and sputters out words like "irregardless," and phrases like "consensus of opinion."

But English is our working language, and we're stuck with it. And all I'm suggesting is that we use it exclusively.

With sincere thanks to Bob Gunning, I once did a Fog Index on a whole pile of church-witten material *(The Technique of Clear Writing,* Robert Gunning. New York: McGraw-Hill, 1952. Buy it! It's probably one of the best investments you as a churchman can make.) Gunning's little system isn't the whole answer, obviously, but it's a pretty good indicator of readability levels. (The Index says that a 12th-grader might have a reading level of 12, a college sophomore 14, and so on. For comparison, my daily newspapers average about 10 on the scale.) The average of my random-sample material from the church was a solid 15, and some of it ran well into the 20's, making it easily understandable to any old Ph.D who's had a few extra years of graduate work tossed in.

The saddest part of all this is that some of the materials were aimed at high-school youth.

Of course there's a built-in risk factor when the author begins Englishing some of this stuff. He runs three distinct risks: First, his manuscript will come out 38 pages short. Second, he might find he has little (if anything) to say. Third, his "oversimplification" might insult his scholar friends, who prefer it a little on the garbled side, with a lot of "transcendentals" thrown in for good measure.

Granted, there's no word that's really synonymous with "resurrection," and there are few words that really mean "salvation." But there are English alternatives to a lot of other words and phrases. Things like "ontological analysis of existence," which comes from a book recommended for us laymen. You've got your choice of what that means:

(a) a medical probe into the soul
(b) a way of using calculus to determine if there's really life on Jupiter
(c) having to do with a Greek god, only the author forgot to capitalize the "O".

Check one and go on to the next paragraph . . . .

Or, if you're still really committed to making sense out of that and countless others like it, try defining it via dictionary, and even rewriting it. My dictionary says ontology is the science of real being; the doctrine of all existence, and so on. It says the word is a philosophical one, a metaphysical one. I say it comes pretty close to being redundant, and if not that, then quite obscure. I suggest that the author try saying something like, "deep look into life," or "serious study of why we're here."

And when he's drummed out of the Christian scholar ranks for not using enough syllables, we'll give him a job in the church.

When you get him working, you can go on to something else. Like churchy study.

(2) *Let's challenge every study we find with a simple set of questions —*

(a) Is what you're studying being studied better elsewhere?

(b) Are you studying for *action*?

(c) If not, will you consider disbanding?

I was guest-preaching at an Ohio church once, when the minister offered me the grand Sunday-morning tour. In one room was a men's Bible class. They were "studying" Amos, and they were engrossed. The average age in that class must have been 55 or 60. Nobody there was younger than 50, I know. The pastor told me that the same group — all ten or so of them — had been meeting consistently for nearly twenty years. You're right: Sunday was the only time they ever got together, and at no time did any mission come out of that group.

The end result of that Bible study was more Bible study, and if that isn't a warped view of study, it'll have to do until another one comes along.

What they did there may be defined in many ways, but study ain't one of them. Not *study* in the Christian sense, anyhow.

Of course the grossest misuse of the word study comes at 9:30 A.M. each Sunday, when most congregations have a "school" in session. I've found that the easiest way to shake them up is to ask questions: "What was it, son, that we learned over the past eight years about the way God acts?" And so forth. There's no intended maliciousness here, just an attempt at getting somebody, somewhere, to see the futility of the standard-brand of Sunday school.

(3) *Try making noise in the church. On a lot of levels, if possible.*

One handy single-word question that will give you a lot of mileage is "Why?" A pastor told me he was working on some new young people in town, who were dropping the kids off on Sunday mornings, but who weren't being reached by the church. When I asked him why, he replied that he wanted to "bring them into the life of the church." And since the church he was pastoring wasn't doing anything in the community I asked him why again, and he could only stare. I don't think he'd ever asked himself that question. Beyond building up the membership rolls, what other purpose would all that effort achieve? I'd have been happy had he told me he was out to offer them salvation, even though I'd have been skeptical. But he couldn't even say that much! Stripped down to its crudest language, I think the guy was blatantly trying to build himself a reputation. And once again, the word *why* is applicable.

Another interesting experiment involves community problems. You can start by asking the pastor if the church is "really interested" in the things that affect men's lives around it. (Don't worry; theologically he almost has to say yes.) When he assures you that it is, start off by giving him some genuine examples of community problems:

— The traffic lights aren't timed on Main Street, and that makes motorists angry, and they take it out on their families.

— There's a man down the street who dropped out of college short of a bachelor's degree, and it's holding him up in his career. Couldn't the church send him back to school?

— Another family (preferably one of a different

religious persuasion) can't afford the luxuries of a freezer or upstairs rugs, but they could if the mother could work, only she has two youngsters at home. Couldn't we organize a reliable babysitting brigade so that she could work for six or eight months?

— The area badly needs a municipal swimming pool. Shouldn't the church build one on the land it owns down the street? No? Then how about asking the community fathers to raise taxes so that one can be built? Still no? Then what if the congregation made a gift to the community in lieu of taxes, and asked that it be earmarked for a pool?

Noisemaking in the sanctuary sometimes gets results, too. One of my biggest disappointments is the regulation sometimes printed at the top of church bulletin covers: "Enter in silence; if you must whisper, whisper a prayer," and so forth. Now a church is made up, it says here, of a *community* of Christ's followers. And community has something to do with fellowship, with knowing the other guy. So a good, bold, loud "Hi there!" in the back of a sanctuary, it would seem, is perfectly in order. Try it daringly, and get that rationale ready for when they come clobbering down on you. (You'll need it.)

Noise *after* the service is best directed at the pastor who just preached a sermon on "involvement" but never offered any concrete ideas about *how* to get involved. He stands at the back of the door, and you make noise: "I didn't hear you say anything about the racial crisis this morning." Try raising your voice a little on the key words.

(4) *Try to get someone fired. (Another form of noise-making.)*

Pick on a Sunday school teacher who's incompetent. Suggest that the church ask him to leave, because he obviously doesn't understand the gospel, and he has no teaching skills. No luck? Then suggest that he be given a course in Christianity and sent to a special class for budding teachers. Still no luck? Then try getting him fired again. Not from the congregation; not from the choir; just from his teaching role.

(5) *Scream (quietly but steadily) for change.*

You'll make a real pest out of yourself if you follow this one, because hardly anyone likes to change anything. But if you search the literature of the church you'll find enough documentation to support your battle. You'll read time and again that it's a changing world, and that "new forms" are needed to cope with it. Okay, what I'm suggesting is that *you suggest* some new forms. Some change. Point out a hymn with an obscure phrase, and demand to know what it means. If people don't know, then suggest that they stop singing it, and get themselves one they can understand. Ditto with other words in the worship service. Challenge the purpose and the effectiveness of the summer Bible school, and the ladies' circles, and the church's outreach program.

Suggest that one volunteer be sent to the local bars on Saturday nights (he can drink ginger ale), to see what need exists. Suggest dialogue sermons, or post-service meetings where you pin the preacher down on the hows and whys of his message. Offer ideas like mid-week breakfast meetings, where community problems can be discussed. Come up with new ways to get the congregation together, like bringing in professional theater groups, or hiring the whole local movie house, and showing a good film. Or suggest closed-circuit TV, using a gifted teacher and a lot of students. Or grades for Sunday school students, complete with tests. Or paid teachers.

The secret is to keep suggesting, offering, prodding, and to get answers each time.

(6) *Fight the long-range planning committee, as well as the shibboleth that function follows form.*

They're first cousins, these two contemporary evils. Long-range planning takes place, and it inevitably leads to a structural appendix that spouts tasks. And it looks backwards from where I sit.

To start with, there is the widely held theory that these changing times demand a "long-range" look ahead, and that seems contradictory in itself. The church is fighting to stay alive under constantly changing climates while segments of it are trying to plot out a temperature line that will be accurate ten years from now. It's one thing to shore up a building in the path of a hurricane; it's quite another to mastermind a full-scale relocation of coastal cities. And if things are really as bad as they look, the master planners had better drop their slide rules and grab sandbags instead.

A football coaching staff plans for an opponent, but when game time arrives they agree on a field quarterback who's prepared to use a flexible offense — changing as the situation demands.

This church team, though, wants to go on running films of past performances while it plots out grand strategy for a game in which the score is already 59-6 in favor of the wrong team.

There is a place for long*er*-range thinking, of course. But it's more of a luxury than we seem ready to admit. And what is particularly frightening is that so many planners grab their slide rules and run when the storm-warning flags go up, instead of helping the church dig in against the elements.

And these planning conferences so often seem to end in *structural* recommendations. That's the corollary evil; we set up more structure — designed to withstand storms we can't even picture yet. And since it's there, erected and staffed, how can it adapt itself to tomorrow's currents? An architect will tell you that you start with the need, and build to suit it. And any competent executive will insist that you define the job, then go get the tools to get it done.

Except in the church.

The church cries on paper and from pulpits, time and again, that "new forms" are needed, "new ways" have to be devised. But it acts out a different story indeed. The "new forms" are acceptable so long as they don't interfere with present forms; the new methods are okay if they don't disturb any current methodology. For decades now the church has been admitting privately that the Sunday school is dead. National magazines have printed articles about the most wasted hour in the week, and almost every churchman of note has recognized the danger. But there are virtually hundreds of task groups in action today planning more structure to accommodate the demon in our midst. And there are mighty few congregations that have faced the failure and been willing to toss structure out the window for something better.

And if you think that the national organizational church is going to change things, you'd better be off buying your own slide rule. Structures perpetuate themselves, and big national structures tend to perpetuate themselves in bigger ways. A new form is going to come from a newly recognized *local* need. In other words, from you.

It's going to bud when you and I take on our own local long-range planners in our own ball park. It's going to bloom and flower when we convince the local ecclesiastical powers that the money ought to be spent for buying sandbags now. One example: A local congregation has 650 members, an average Sunday worship attendance of 200, and little or no impact on the community. It's an acculturated house of worship, instead of a gospel-oriented bastion for God and man. Now: is this any time to plan for a new sanctuary? To set up a committee that will reorganize the choir? To take an option on the property next door?

Or is this the time to clean up the membership rolls, examine the life of the church, and dig in for an obviously tough battle ahead?

How? By raising the issues as they stand now, honestly, and by speaking up. If you're looking for a palliative that will keep everybody happy, you've wasted your money on the wrong book. Which leads us to a final recommendation:

(7) *Let's take the risk of splitting the church, if necessary.*

As I understand it, there were people who didn't particularly care for what Jesus was saying. After all, it was rather threatening, wasn't it? I mean loving God beyond nation, beyond self. And showing that love toward people who hated their guts. But what has happened in between? Where did this movement pick up the overriding doctrine that there's room for anybody in Christ's church?

New Testament people proclaimed, all right. But when their message was rejected did they dilute it to fit the world? Or did they stick with it in the original?

Contrast that with today's church — with that 650-member congregation above, if you will. How many of those members would you say have rejected the gospel? Half? Two-thirds? How many join without accepting? Nine-tenths? When membership time comes round, what are the criteria? A watered-down speech? A meeting at which they have to recite some key phrases?

To me, membership in the organized form of Christ's believing body does not start with enrollment and then go on to basic training. Enrollment is commitment, and nothing short of that will do. The basic training — the proclamation and interpretation — comes first. Commitment can only be made to a basic principle. Then we get on to things like nurture.

This is not to challenge those who profess commitment: I'd be presumptuous not to stop short of that. But I would challenge our methods of building-by-the-numbers, our way of adding members.

And I think that any genuine reform is soon going to have the effect of a new proclamation toward those who haven't committed themselves. It's at that point that reform bogs down. It's there that we're inclined to worry more about the "unity" of the church than about its centrality. And it's here that I run scared. Because I'm outnumbered, that's why.

I remember sitting on a local-church governing body once and trying to help pare down the membership rolls. Some "members" hadn't been near the place for years. But when the time came to scratch their names, there were those who insisted that we couldn't shut the church doors to anyone. As if we were barring them from worship!

Participation is one thing. Membership is another thing. And maybe a good sharp knife is needed to separate the two.

All of the above is going to take courage. Probably more courage than I've got. But if you and I start out *together*, who knows how many others we can recruit? Providing we take it seriously, of course.

And speaking of things that people won't take seriously: Have you heard the one about God becoming man? . . .